Dropping In On...
AUSTRALIA

Lewis K. Parker

A Geography Series

ROURKE BOOK COMPANY, INC.
VERO BEACH, FLORIDA 32964

A Blackbirch Graphics book.

Printed in the United States of America.

Library of Congress Cataloging-in-Publication Data

Parker, Lewis K.
    Australia / Lewis K. Parker.
        p.   cm. — (Dropping in on)
    Includes bibliographic references and index.
    ISBN 1-55916-007-1
    1. Australia—Description and travel—Juvenile literature. [1. Australia—Description and travel.] I. Title. II. Series: Parker, Lewis K. Dropping in on.
    DU105.2.P37   1994
    994—dc20   94-4249
                                                CIP
                                                AC

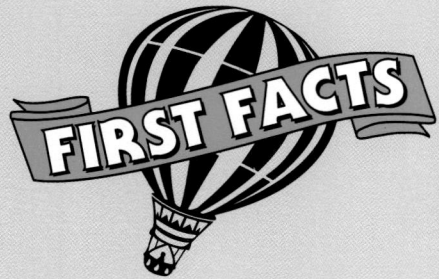

FIRST FACTS

Australia

Official Name: Commonwealth of Australia

Area: 2,966,150 square miles

Population: 17,800,000

Capital: Canberra

Largest City: Sydney

Highest Elevation: Mt. Kosciusko (7,310 feet)

Official Language: English

Major Religions: Protestant and Roman Catholic

Money: Australian Dollar

Form of Government: Parliamentary Democracy

TABLE OF CONTENTS

Our Blue Ball—The Earth

The Earth can be divided into two hemispheres. The word hemisphere means "half a ball"—in this case, the ball is the Earth.

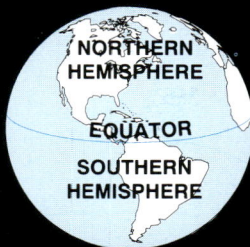

The equator is an imaginary line that runs around the middle of the Earth. It separates the Northern Hemisphere from the Southern Hemisphere. North America—where Canada, the United States, and Mexico are located—is in the Northern Hemisphere.

The Southern Hemisphere

When the South Pole is tilted toward the sun, the sun's most powerful rays strike the southern half of the Earth and less sunshine hits the Northern Hemisphere. That is when people in the Southern Hemisphere enjoy summer. When the

South Pole is tilted away from the sun, and the Northern Hemisphere receives the most sunshine, the seasons reverse. Then winter comes to the Southern Hemisphere. The seasons in the Southern Hemisphere and the Northern Hemisphere are always opposite. Australia is in the Southern Hemisphere.

Indian Ocean

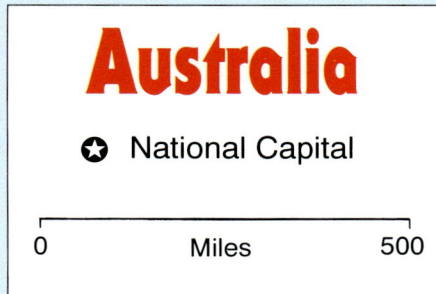

Australia

⭐ National Capital

0   Miles   500

STOP 4

WESTERN
AUSTRALIA

Get Ready for Australia

STOP 5

Perth

Hop into your hot air balloon. Let's take a trip!

Australia is the world's largest island. It is the only country that is also a continent. It is about the size of the mainland United States. The population of Australia is about 18 million, which is almost the same as the population of New York State.

The name Australia means "southern place." It is often called "the land down under" because it is below the equator in the Southern Hemisphere.

STOP 2

Gulf of Carpentaria

Coral Sea

GREAT BARRIER REEF

Great Sandy Desert

NORTHERN TERRITORY

STOP 3

■ **Ayers Rock**

QUEENSLAND

SOUTH AUSTRALIA

STOP 6

STOP 1

NEW SOUTH WALES

Canberra ✪

Sydney

Indian Ocean

VICTORIA

Melbourne

STOP 7

STOP 8

TASMANIA

Stop 1: Sydney

We'll begin our Australia visit in Sydney. This city, which is on the southeast coast, is the largest city in Australia. About 4 million people live here.

Sydney is a busy city with tall buildings and a very beautiful harbor. In the streets, you'll see musicians, singers, and jugglers.

An important stop is the Sydney Opera House, which faces the harbor. This unusual-looking opera house has a roof that resembles sails, seashells, or birds' wings, depending on how you look at it. The roofs are made up of thousands of white tiles.

The Harbor Bridge is near the opera house. The bridge is frequently called "the Coathanger" because it looks like a coat hanger.

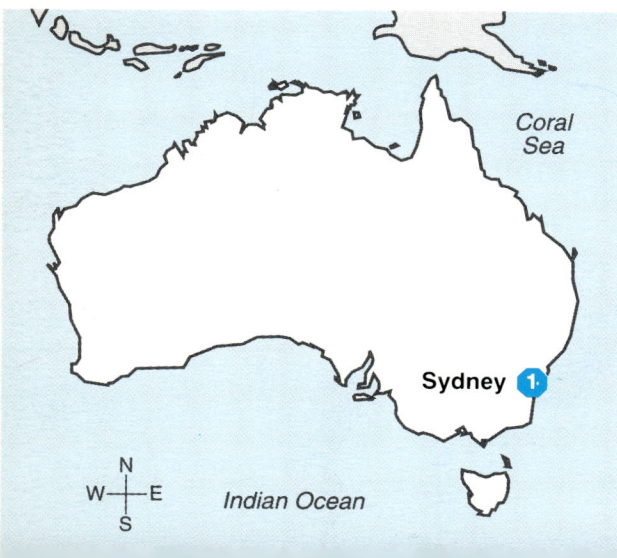

Opposite: Boats on the harbor cruise by the Sydney Opera House. Here, visitors can see concerts, movies, and plays, as well as operas.

*Now let's fly **north** to the Great Barrier Reef.*

Stop 2: The Great Barrier Reef

The Great Barrier Reef is the longest string of coral reefs in the world. It stretches about 1,250 miles along the east coast of Australia in the Coral Sea. That is about the same length as the west coast of the United States from Mexico to Canada.

The Great Barrier Reef was formed thousands of years ago. During low tide, you can see through the crystal-clear water to the coral below.

Many kinds of sea animals live among the coral. Sea cucumbers are common, as are blue and red starfish. Giant clams that weigh more than 150 pounds, green turtles that are 3 feet across, and other sea creatures make the coral their home.

Opposite: A scuba diver reaches out to tropical fish in the Great Barrier Reef. Many kinds of coral and sea animals live here.

Coral
Sea

Great
Barrier
Reef

Indian Ocean

Next, we'll travel **west** to Ayers Rock.

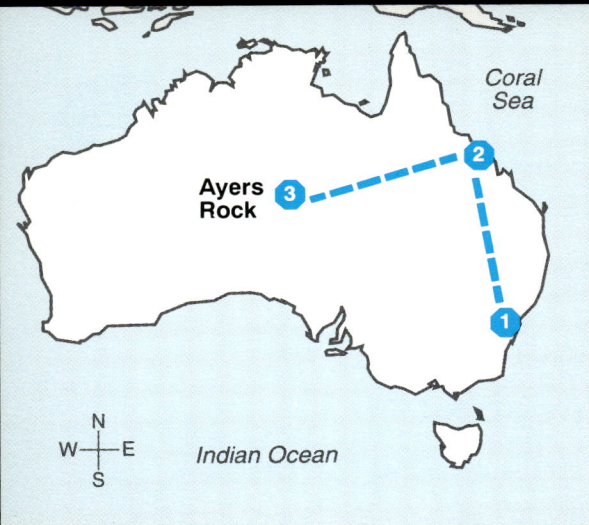

Stop 3: Ayers Rock

Ayers Rock is a natural sandstone tower in the Northern Territory that is a half mile around at its base and 2 miles wide. It rises more than 1,000 feet above the flat earth.

Ayers Rock is called *Uluru* by the Aborigines. They are the native people of Australia. They consider the rock a sacred place. It is very easy to

Ayers Rock glows red in the sunlight. Its red color comes from a layer of rusty dust on its surface.

understand the Aborigines' belief when you see the rock. It changes color as rays of the sun strike it from sunrise to sunset. It slowly turns from a reddish color to a deeper red, and seems to glow from within before it fades to black. The next morning, it begins as a gray slab, and slowly changes over the day to deep red again. Ayers Rock is in a part of Australia often called "the bush."

The Aborigines

The native inhabitants of Australia are called Aborigines. There are about 200,000 Aborigines in Australia. About half of these people live in cities and towns. The rest live and work on cattle and sheep stations, or on their own land.

Aborigines can survive in barren wilderness areas where there are few plants and no water. Some Aborigines who live in the wilderness, or "bush," wear little clothing. They often wear only a *naga*, or loincloth. Aborigines in the "bush" usually live in shelters made of branches—however, some live in houses.

Aborigines speak a language that has many clicking sounds. Here are some of their words:

Anangu	the people (Aborigines)
Kapi	water
Malu	a kangaroo
Nguru	home

Now let's sail **northwest** to the Great Sandy Desert.

Aborigines in the Northern Territory hold a traditional dance. Uluru, Ayers Rock, can be seen in the distance.

Stop 4: The Great Sandy Desert

The Great Sandy Desert is an enormous desert in Western Australia. Australians call much of the eastern central area of this state "the outback." The Great Sandy Desert is hot and dry. Some of the lakes in this desert are dry for many years at a time. About 2,000 Aborigines live in the Great Sandy Desert.

Further south, the Pinnacles Desert is a flat, sandy area that has strange limestone rocks. This desert often looks like a forest of rust-colored rocks. From August to October, wildflowers bloom throughout the desert, making it come alive with the colors of the rainbow.

*Now let's fly **southwest** to Perth.*

Coral
Sea

Great
Sandy
Desert

N
W—E
S

Indian Ocean

The Great Sandy
Desert is a vast desert
in Western Australia
that is home to very
few people. Inset:
Large limestone rocks
make up the landscape
in the Pinnacles
Desert.

Stop 5: Perth

Perth, a major seaport by the Indian Ocean, is the largest city in Western Australia. In front of the Perth Town Hall is a tower of minerals. This tower represents the mineral wealth of Western Australia. Many minerals and gems are mined in this area.

Because of Perth's location, it is a major fishing center, specializing in shrimp and lobster.

A Visit to a Sheep Station

In Australia, there are 9 times as many sheep as there are people. Australia has about 80,000 sheep stations where the sheep are raised and then sheared, or shaved, for their wool.

A worker shears wool at a sheep station.

Sheep are sheared during mustering time, an annual roundup of the sheep during the hottest time of the year. Shearing keeps the sheep cool and keeps ticks and lice off of them.

Workers herd the sheep down to a shearing shed. There, a shearer uses mechanical clippers to cut off the wool. First, the shearer clips the worthless wool along the belly and the inside of the legs. Next, the excellent wool on the sheep's back, called a fleece, is removed in one piece. One fleece may weigh about 10 pounds.

*Now let's hop in our balloon and swing **southeast** to Victoria.*

Stop 6: Victoria

This southern area of Australia contains more than 4 million people. It has flat plains stretching westward and mountains in its north. Along the coast, the view is spectacular with huge rocks and pounding waves.

The mountains are called the Victorian Alps. They are part of the Great Dividing Range. This range of mountains separates the fertile coast from the interior. The Victorian Alps are prized for skiing. Mt. Hotham and Mt. Buller are considered excellent for this sport.

The southeast region of Victoria is called Gippsland. This area receives enough rainfall to

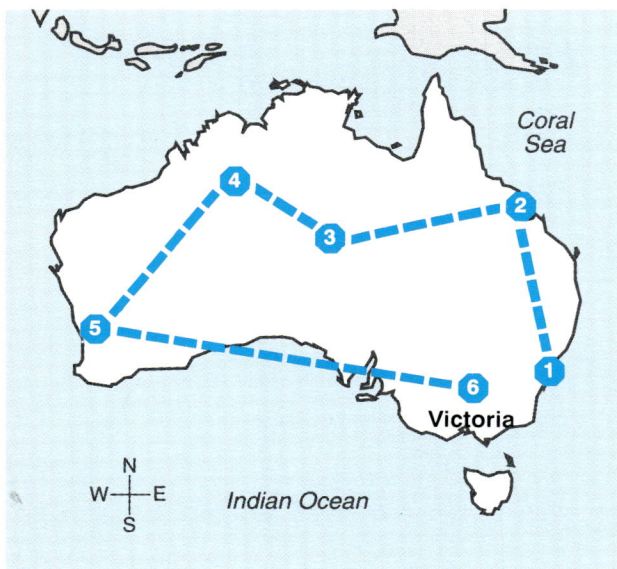

Opposite: The Victorian Alps are covered with snow and are great for skiing during the winter. In the summer, visitors can enjoy hiking, camping, and rafting in these mountains.

be a fertile area for farming. Wheat and fruit are grown here. Large coal deposits have been found in Gippsland, as well. Also, three major rivers create a huge lake system here.

💧 *Now we'll travel* **south** *to Melbourne, the capital city of Victoria.*

Stop 7: Melbourne

About 3 million people live in Melbourne, the capital of Victoria. This city has both wide boulevards lined with gardens and straight streets that sometimes turn into narrow alleys. The Yarra River runs along the southern side of the city. There are many parks, walkways, and bike trails along the banks of the river.

Just south of Melbourne you can visit Phillip Island. This island is the home of fairy penguins. These little penguins spend all day in the ocean hunting for fish. At night, they waddle up on shore and walk in single-file to burrow into their nests. Floodlights are set up on the beach so that visitors can watch the penguins' parade.

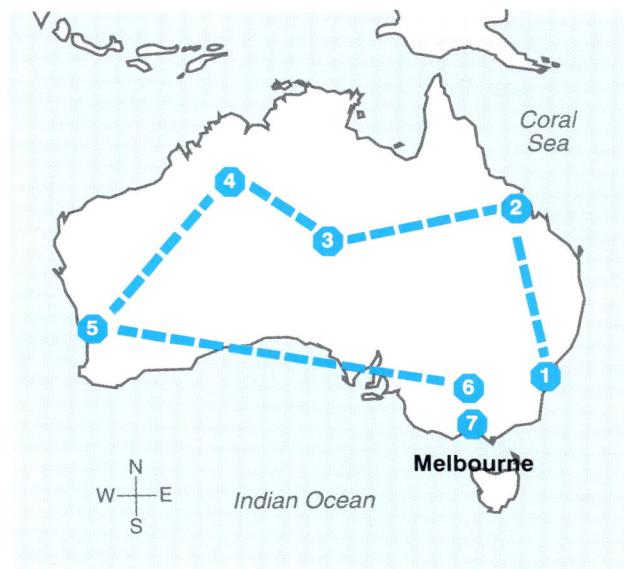

Opposite:
The South Gate
crosses the Yarra
River in downtown
Melbourne.

A frilled lizard flares its collar and shows its colors.

Animals of Australia

A kookaburra.

Australia is famous for its unusual animals, some of which are not found anywhere else. Australia has a variety of marsupials—mammals that have pouches in which they carry their young. The best-known marsupial is the kangaroo. Some kangaroos weigh 185 pounds, can jump 28 feet in a single bound, and can run 50 miles per hour. Koalas carry their newborn babies in pouches, but later the babies ride on their mothers' backs.

Australia also has strange birds and reptiles. The emu is a huge bird that can't fly. Kookaburras have a loud cry that sounds like wild laughter. The frilled lizard, a reptile, has a collar around its neck. The collar flares out when the lizard is threatened by another animal.

Below left: A kangaroo stops for a rest in Western Australia. Below right: A koala sits in a eucalyptus tree, eating the leaves.

*For our final stop, let's fly **southeast** to Tasmania, an island off the coast of Australia.*

Stop 8: Tasmania

A Tasmanian devil.

Tasmania is a heart-shaped island about 150 miles off the southeast coast of Australia. Tasmania is mountainous, has heavy rainfall, and has 4,000 lakes. Most of the people live on the north and southeast coasts, where the land is rich and fertile.

The southwest and west receive a lot of rain, and, as a result, rainforests have developed there. The rainforest is so thick that the light coming through the trees is pale green. The rainforest has sassafras trees, eucalyptus trees, and giant trees that are thousands of years old. The Tasmanian devil, a marsupial, lives here. These animals are mean and look it. Their powerful jaws and sharp teeth allow them to easily chew through bone.

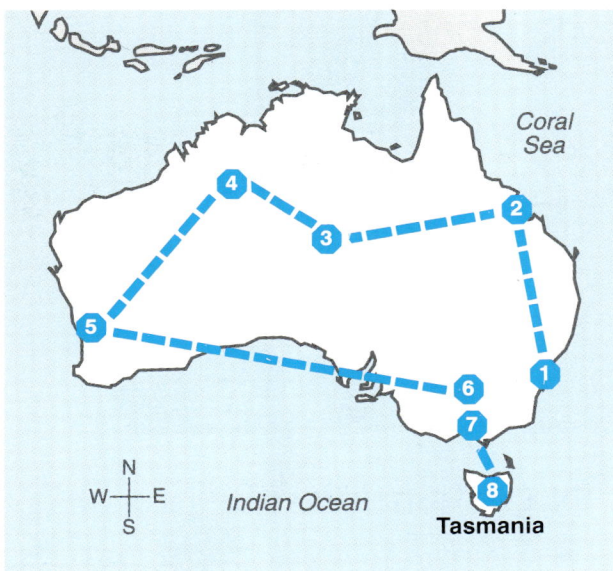

Coral Sea

Indian Ocean

Tasmania

A stream flows through St. Columbia Walk rainforest in Tasmania.

Now it's time to set sail for home. When you return, you can think back on the wonderful adventure you had in Australia.

Aussie Language

People in Australia speak English. They also have their own way of using the language. Many words have special meanings. Here is a list of some Aussie words.

Aussie Words	What They Mean
bail out	leave
barbie	barbeque
bathers	swimsuits
beg yours	I beg your pardon
bikkies	biscuits (cookies)
burl	have a try
chips	french fries
chook	chicken
crisps	potato chips
daks	trousers
earbash	talk nonstop
grouse	very good
icy-pole	popsicle
lolly water	soft drink
no worries	no problem
yahoo	noisy person

Further Reading

Browne, Rollo. *A Family in Australia*. Minneapolis, MN: Lerner, 1987.

_____. *An Aboriginal Family*. Minneapolis, MN: Lerner, 1985.

Conforth, Kellie. *A Picture Book of Australian Animals*. Mahwah, NJ: Troll, 1992.

Georges, D. V. *Australia*. Chicago, IL: Childrens Press, 1986.

James, Ian. *Australia*. New York: Franklin Watts, 1989.

Mattern, Joanne. *Australian Animals*. Mahwah, NJ: Troll, 1993.

Powzyk, Joyce. *Wallaby Creek*. New York: Lothrop, 1985.

Index

Acknowledgments and Photo Credits
Cover and page 23: ©Bill Bachman/Photo Researchers, Inc.; pp. 4, 6:
National Aeronautics and Space Administration; pp. 11, 12, 14, 16, 18, 20,
21, 24, 26, 27, 29: ©Australian Tourist Commission; p. 19: ©Alain Buu/
Liaison International (inset); p. 28: ©Jack S. Grove/Liaison International.
Maps by Blackbirch Graphics, Inc.